BEAUTY FOR ASHES

RUVA NGUNDU

BEAUTY FOR ASHES

ISBN-13 :9781521946725

Cover art by Bentley Francis Shomai

Dedication

This book is dedicated to every woman and girl who is struggling with the battle of the mind and soul ties. This book is also dedicated to the young/teen single mothers who think and feel all hope is lost and gone because they had a baby/child out of wedlock.

My prayer for you is that as you read this book, may your heart not be hardened to receive God's love. When you hear His voice as you read this book, harden not your heart. No matter what has happened to you, He promised in His word that if you return to Him, He will build you up (Job 22:23)

Table of Contents

Acknowledgements 5

Introduction Page 6

Chapter 1 Page 9

Chapter 2 Page 12

Chapter 3 Page 17

Chapter 4 Page 20

Chapter 5 Page 25

Conclusion Page 37

Acknowledgements

My first acknowledgement goes to God who has shown Himself to be so faithful to His promise that "If you return to The Almighty, you will be built up." - Job 22:23" Without Him, there is no me. I love Him so much.

My Parents - For supporting me in all I do and for praying for and with me, thank you.

My Siblings -You are my joy! I love you guys

My Bishop - Bishop H Muzhari and Mum Muzhari, who could ask for a better Bishop and mum? If I ever had to repick, I would pick you guys again. Thank you for praying for and with me.

Finally, my church family - I am excited about our future, it's very bright!

Introduction

My name is Ruva, meaning "flower" in Shona. My full name is "Ruvarashe" which means "flower of God." I was born on the 25th of July 1989 in Harare, Zimbabwe. I am the first of 3 children of Pastor D.N. Ngundu and Mrs E.C. Ngundu. I moved to United Kingdom on the 7th of January 2001. I was 12 years old then and I still reside in UK to this day. My home church is Family Covenant Church, which is being led by The Holy Spirit through His Servant, Bishop H. Muzhari.

We have quite a number of FCC (Family Covenant Church) branches all over UK, Africa and Australia. My dad is the Pastor of Family Covenant Church here in London. I was raised in church but I received Jesus Christ in my heart and in my life as my Lord and Saviour on the 24th of August 2004, aged 15. I was baptised and filled with The Holy Spirit on the 29th of September of the same year.

I had an idea of what "being saved" was. Yes, I went to all the Sunday Services, went to all the Wednesday night bible studies, had all the holy communions etc. but, there came a time in my life where I had to get salvation for myself. Yes, your parents can pray for you, lay hands on you, anoint you etc. but, when it comes to salvation, you are going to have to get it by yourself and for yourself!

That's why the bible says in Philippians 2:12, *"Therefore my beloved, as you have always obeyed, not as in my presence only, but now much more in my absence, work out your own salvation with fear and trembling."*

It does not say, "work out the salvation that you received from your parents, pastors, bishops etc. no. Instead, it says, "work out YOUR OWN salvation with fear and trembling" so that you don't only obey in the presence of your parents or leaders, but also, you'll be able to obey when your parents or leaders are not around. If you only obey when your parents or leaders are present, then it means that you need to work out your salvation with fear and trembling to a point where The Holy Spirit will dwell in you so comfortably that if you think of disobeying/sinning, He will convict you very strongly.

Be careful if you ever get to a point where you sin (knowingly or unknowingly) and you don't feel "some type of way" about it.

A frog is an amphibian. An amphibian is a cold blooded vertebrate animal. If you put a frog into boiling water, it will jump out. However, if you put a frog in cold water and slowly raise up the temperature to cook it, because a frog is cold blooded, it can adjust to the temperature. It will not realise the change in the temperature, what the frog doesn't know is it's being cooked. By the time the frog realises this, it will be too late.

Likewise, each time you sin and there's no conviction which leads to repentance, you're like that frog that's being cooked slowly but unaware.

Chapter One
If you leave the door open, the devil will come in.

Ephesians 4:27 "do not give the devil a foothold."

If we give the enemy a foothold in our lives and if we don't deal with it then that foothold will become a stronghold which will be much harder to break. Dealing with this means firstly recognising that the enemy has gained a foothold in your life and then after you recognise it:

- you bind and rebuke him and seal every door, window and avenue into your life with the blood of Jesus
- also taking inventory of your life and asking God, *"okay, I have rebuked and cast the devil out but Lord, reveal to me how he got in in the first place? And what must I do to make sure that when he comes back again, he won't be able to get in?"*

So, yes it's very important to know the enemy's devices and schemes.

When it came to me, the enemy wanted to destroy my parents because of the anointing that's on their lives. When the enemy came, he saw that he couldn't get to my parents so he tried to destroy my parents through me, their first born. My dad always refers to me as "the beginning of my strength", therefore, the enemy intentionally attacked me in order to weaken my parents.

Hear me and hear me well guys, if the enemy can't get your parents, he will get to your parents through you or the next closest thing. Or maybe, just maybe, the enemy will just be after you because it's your seed that will crush the head of the serpent. The fact that you have a great destiny and purpose also makes the enemy very angry and his mission is always to kill, steal and destroy… he wants nothing left of you!

The devil can enter anyone who gives him access and permission. The devil is a spirit and just like God he needs a vehicle (which is a body) to operate through to carry out his plans. Don't be surprised how far the enemy will go to try and stop you and also, don't be surprised who he may use to try and stop you.
I became blind to the fact and truth that my parents love me and they always will. That's what the enemy does when he wants to attack any child of God. The enemy will try to get you to come out of your place of protection, just like he did to the prodigal son, but we thank God that he came back to his senses.
My mum had told my dad that "something was not right" and my mum was right,

something was definitely not right. Right now you're probably thinking "why didn't you tell your parents?" Well, the honest truth to that question is fear. Like I said at the beginning, the relationship I had with my parents had been tampered with, which then opened up the door to a lot of things because I was out of my place of protection and seeds were sown into me to make it look like my parents were my enemy.

I knew something was wrong because my monthly cycle stopped and I gained weight excessively. I went for a blood test and I waited for the results. After 2 weeks of not getting a reply from them, I called my GP and I told her *"I came to get my bloods taken and I've still not gotten my results."* She screamed on the phone and said *"we're looking for you with red eyes!!"* I said *"oh really? Is everything okay?"* then she said *"are you able to come and see me today"* then I said *"yeah sure."* This was on Thursday the 25th of August 2011.

One of my aunts Mrs. C offered to come with me and I said okay. When I got in the room, the GP looked at me and said *"you don't have fibroids, you're pregnant, that's what's happening."* My head started spinning in disbelief as I said *"no!! it can't be!"* Then she said *"well you are my love, so what are you going to do?"* then I said *"well, I'm a Christian, abortion is out of the picture. I will keep my child."* That's when the warfare started

Chapter Two

It all starts in the mind.

The first thing that we did when me and my aunt got back home was to seriously pray. I repented and I just gave the whole issue to God. That night when I went to bed, I literally saw a creature with a hoodie and then I became weak and the creature lifted up its finger and that finger became a HUGE claw and the creature started stabbing my brain.

The following morning I woke up thinking all kinds of negative stuff about myself. I started battling with thoughts of suicide, condemnation, guilt, discouragement and low self-esteem. I was so angry at God. I remember writing a very nasty cruel letter to God swearing at Him, telling Him how much I hated Him, how I never want to see or speak to Him ever again, how I wanted to hurt Him because He hurt me and I also told God that I wasn't going to worship Him until He *"fixes my life and does what I want"*

The manner in which I behaved can be likened to a wife who withholds sex from her husband because he has wronged her. I withheld my worship and praise from God to the point where I was numb to God's presence. I didn't pray or talk to God for 2 years.

The mind is a battlefield. God took me on a journey of renewing of my mind. During that time, I took time off ministering and everything. I took time to go to God and seek Him and to hear God for myself. I remember saying to God *"Lord, you spoke to Samuel when he was young, you spoke to Jeremiah when he was young, you said your sheep hear your voice, and the voice of a stranger they will not follow, I am one of your sheep so I have that right and privilege to be able to hear your voice."*

I didn't want to go to a Prophet or anyone else to hear from God through them or to receive a prophetic word. Have you ever played Chinese Whispers? When the message passes through 5 people…by the time the message gets to you, it would have been diluted, so it's better to go to the Source. In this case, God was my source. We are living in the last days and it is dangerous not only for you as a woman, girl, and lady but as a Christian to not hear from God. If faith can come just by hearing, then it paramount for you to be able to hear from your creator. It is also dangerous to just do and say anything without the leadership and the guidance of The Holy Spirit.

"Those who are led by The Spirit of God, these are the Sons of God." Romans 8:14

The battle of the mind is something that God has helped me with.

When your mind and your thinking is out of control and if it doesn't line up with God's word and you're double minded, it hinders you from receiving from God according to James 1:6-8. So, you need to start thinking about what you're thinking about. You can't allow the enemy to control your mind in such a way that it becomes normal to you.

You can't allow it to get to a stage where you are no longer aware of what you are thinking about. There will be so many things, thoughts, reasoning and imaginations running wild through your mind, even the devil will give you suggestions, ideas and reasoning. At some point you will start considering those ideas which then means you have allowed the enemy to plant his thoughts and his ideas in the incubator of your mind. The more you meditate on those ideas and suggestion, the more they will grow.

The bible says in 2nd Corinthians 10:5, *"We destroy sophisticated arguments, reasonings and every exalted and proud thing that sets itself up against the true knowledge of God, and we also take every thought captive to the obedience of Jesus Christ."*

The place where victory is obtained in your life is based on how you think.

"As a man thinketh in his heart so is he." Proverbs 23:7

In other words, he is in his heart the way he thinks in his mind. If your thinking is not in line with God's word, then your thinking is in line with something else, and that alone is very dangerous. The standard of our thoughts as Christians or as children of God must be based on the word of God. Start thinking about what you're thinking about (Philippians 4:8). Sober thinking is when your thinking and your mind-set is in line with God's word.

The first thing that happened in this whole journey was that I had to recognise when my thinking was out of control and I had to quickly take captive of that thought and all these imaginations and reasoning that were not in line with God's word. I had to replace them with the truth of God's word.

"Sanctify them by the truth, for thy word is truth ."
John 17:17

I replaced them by speaking the truth of God's word out loud over my life and over myself. You can't just sit there quietly like a trained puppy waiting for the owner to give it orders. Fight back/Talk back to the devil. The only way the enemy will be quiet is if you say something worth shutting up to.

Don't allow the enemy to run his mouth on you whilst you have yours shut. There's power in your words. Use them! Jesus did the same.

When the enemy came to Jesus to tempt Him, Jesus did not keep His mouth shut. He fought back with the word. So, when you realise that your thinking is out of control, immediately confront it. If you have any negative thought whether "big" or "small" make sure you don't let that thought linger in your mind, confront it immediately with the word of God.

The Word hidden in my heart is to keep my flesh in line, the word in my mouth is to keep the enemy in line and under control.

You can't confront the enemy without the word of God dwelling richly inside of you. So, as the bible says in Colossians 3:16,

"Let the word of God dwell richly inside you."

In closing, Isaiah 26:3 God promises to keep us in perfect peace if we keep our mind stayed on Him. Meaning, your mind must lean on Him, centre on Him and trust Him. Your tranquility of mind is perfect or imperfect to the degree that your mind is stayed on Him. Therefore, keep your mind stayed on God at all times, thereby you will be kept in perfect peace.

Chapter Three

Soul ties

If you knew how powerful sex was you wouldn't have it with just anybody. During sex there are two different exchanges that take place: 1. physical and 2. spiritual. Most grown adults are aware of the physical exchange, but the second is the spiritual which most people don't know about.

When you have sex with someone, you exchange/ obtain whatever spirit(s) they have as well. You take on their qualities , behaviors, ideologies etc. Good or bad, you take them & they become a part of you.

Sex was intended for one man and one woman. So many problems come as a result of sex outside of marriage. Disease and unplanned pregnancy are just the tip of an iceberg. You enter into a covenant with that other person's spirit. This happens every time you have sex with someone. In addition to this, whoever they have had sex with before you, you now become attached to those people's spirits as well. This is why there are so many people with multiple personalities, dibbling and dabbling in this and that, confused and all messed up in their thoughts, feelings and behavior. They are dealing with their own personality as well as the other people they have physically and spiritually connected themselves to.

How can this be avoided? Do it God's way. Just wait. Save sex until marriage. God knows how it feels and what it does. He created it! But, he also put boundaries in place because He knew what would happen when people are careless with it. The good news is this doesn't have to be you. If you haven't already engaged in sexual activity then don't. Save it for your husband or wife. If you have, don't do it anymore. Ask God for discipline.

The bible says in proverbs 25:28 anyone who lacks self control is like a house with its doors and windows knocked out. Anything goes! Take your pick. Either run the risk of sleeping with the enemy or wait and be in the ark of safety in marriage.

Let's commit to setting physical boundaries long before we get into a relationship. By knowing where you stand and what God has called you to do, you'll be stronger and less likely to give into temptation when it comes.

It's easy to decide to commit to purity. It's more difficult to follow through.

Ambiguity is one of the leading causes of moral failure - you don't make the right decision because you haven't decided what the right decision is! A lot of us don't take the time to process how we feel or what God has told us is within His will for us physically. It's no wonder that when we're in tempting situations, we cave.

Without knowing your own boundaries, it's easy to blame the other person for 'pushing your boundaries' or 'doing more than you would have wanted.' Instead of making excuses, it's time to own your purity. Decide how God wants you to live and be bold! Share your thoughts with your boyfriend or girlfriend early on and build accountability within your relationship, as well as with other trusted friends. Don't wait until you've gone too far and feel guilty to determine your boundaries. Don't wait until you hit the other person's boundaries. Take initiative to protect your purity and your significant other's purity. Your relationship with Jesus and your ability to hear His voice will grow stronger when you realise that purity starts with you.

• Spend some time listing out 5-10 physical boundaries that you need to have. These need to be as honest and specific as possible. For example, we should not hang out in each other's bedrooms alone? etc.

.You're not DELIVERED from SIN until you're DELIVERED from the

RESIDUE of it! The RESIDUE can and will grow into what you once you thought you were delivered from!

Chapter Four

Don't awaken love Before Its Time.

"Daughters of Jerusalem, I charge you by the gazelles and by the hinds of the field, do not awaken love until the time is right."
Songs of Solomon 2:7

Pre-marital sex brings demons, real scary demons that you see out of the corner of your eye or stand in the doorway of your bedroom. 12 June 2012 is a day I will never forget. A creature appeared in my dream and it looked at me so angrily and furiously. It then started looking at me up and down, sizing me up. This caused me to have insomnia, depression, tremendous fear and suicidal thoughts. I remember literally dreading to go to bed because the enemy had his grip on me super tight.

Afterwards, I then started seeking for validation, love, peace and acceptance in the wrong place. That wrong place was called masturbation.

When we use the powerful force of imagining something as if it were real, we are actually attracting that which we imagine into physical being. When we imagine having sex with another person via masturbation, we are actually summoning that which we are imagining. In the spirit world and according to Matthew 5:8, the sexual thought is the same as the sexual act. Masturbation is a demonic spirit, and the danger in masturbating is that one could inadvertently summon other demons to attach themselves to you through the act of masturbating. Once that demon attaches itself to you, it is difficult for it to leave. It will drive you to masturbate even when you don't want to. The force for you to masturbate will be so strong that only an orgasm will allow you some temporal relief.

In worst case scenarios, that one demon may gather other unclean spirits to also attach themselves to your life, that way it can wrap you tighter in its web of control, making it that much more difficult for you to get free and many never find their freedom. (Matthew 12:43-45).

By engaging in acts of sexual impurity, you are giving evil spirits legal access into your life which will cause trauma, pain, guilt and shame. You have to fast and pray and genuinely ask God to help you because some stuff (including masturbation) only come out through prayer and fasting.

Also talk to someone about it, whether an Apostle, Prophet, Evangelist or a Pastor, just ensure you are led by The Holy Spirit when choosing who you should talk to. The Bible refers to this as bearing one another's burdens.

The next thing you must do is to have self-control. If you know that watching certain stuff is going to arouse you or should I say "awaken love" then don't watch it. If you know that certain conversations will arouse you, don't entertain the conversations, walk out, flee or politely say *"I'm not comfortable having this conversation."* If you know that going to certain places or being at certain places is going to trigger your hormones, then don't go there! Be disciplined! Have self-control.

If you know that at night you watch pornography or you masturbate, don't sleep near your phone or you can give your phone to one of your family members e.g. mum or dad if you live with them. Don't give the devil any room! There's no *"I'm going to watch porn just this one time."* When you watch porn, it's going to be hard to stop. You have to make a covenant with your eyes that you will not watch pornography or any sexually explicit movies, TV shows or videos on the internet. There's no such thing as *"soft porn"* or *"I'll just watch mild porn, it's nothing serious."* If you give the enemy an inch, he will be your ruler. There's no innocent *"white sin"* that doesn't give the kingdom of hell rights and authority over your life.

Yes you can bind and rebuke the enemy, however don't reopen the door because the devil is roaming around like a roaring lion watching and waiting for an opening. So honour God with what you watch.

Psalms 101:3, *"I will set no worthless or wicked thing before my eyes. I hate the practice of those who fall away from the right path, it will not grasp hold of me."*

So, self-control is very important. It is one of the fruits of The Holy Spirit. Marriage doesn't cure lust, if it did, adultery wouldn't exist. Marriage doesn't cure masturbation. There are a lot of married men and married women who masturbate. The worst thing to do is to view marriage as a sex release. It doesn't matter if you are single or married, **you may be Solomon in wisdom, David in praise and worship, Abraham in faith or Joshua in war, but if you are not Joseph in discipline and in self-control, you will end up like Samson in destruction.**

If you're struggling with masturbation you're not alone. Masturbation is definitely a sin. I know some of you who are reading are saying *"well it's not in the bible, give us a verse! The bible says thou shall not kill, steal, lie etc. but it doesn't say thou shall not masturbate"* If I didn't know any better I would agree with you. But, before I continue, please answer this question for me, *"can you masturbate to the point of having an orgasm without lust being part of that experience?"*

The answer is NO. The enemy wants to take advantage of our ignorance because after all even God said in Hosea 4:6, *"My people perish because of lack of knowledge."* We are not harmed or destroyed by anything that devil or this world can do or ever come up with, we are destroyed because we lack knowledge and the enemy is taking FULL advantage of it.

Chapter Five
How Satan Controls Your Mind.

Deliverance is not only Spiritual, but it's also emotional. You have to take care of your emotional gates. Our emotional gates are very much mental. It comes from where our memories are held, things that we have experienced and how it affects us or how it has affected us. The enemy will use even natural things to have spiritual control over your mind. So, if you've had experiences where you've been disappointed, someone failed you, someone bullied you, you were sexually molested, raped by your dad, uncle, brother or anyone who may or not be close to you, it's important that you seek healing in those moments and not let it sit. The longer you let it sit and the longer you don't seek healing or speak to someone, the tighter the grip the enemy has over you.

According to 2 Timothy 1:7, God has given us the gift of a sound mind. You have to speak that over yourself. Don't allow what has happened to you to cause you to be emotionally imbalanced.

The enemy controls our mind through lack of confidence and fear based thoughts. Fear based thoughts are things like low self- esteem, doubt and going back and forth on things you want to do (double mindedness). Anger is also a fear based thought because anger resides in the bosom of a fool. A lot of times that anger turns into offense which then can turn into insecurity. So, we can't hold onto a spirit of offense or anger. These things have to be resolved quickly.

That's why Jesus said we must forgive people regularly, 70 times 7 times because if we don't, the enemy will literally set us up in the area which we have allowed him to come in.

Therefore, I had to forgive my dad's best friend and I had to forgive myself. Forgiveness is to release pain. Forgiveness is saying *"I release these things that are negative so that I can retain my peace."*

"Follow peace with all man."
Hebrews 12:14

That is a requirement. That is also part of keeping your emotional health intact. The person that has mastered being emotionally balanced is the person that has mastered forgiveness. If you haven't mastered forgiveness then you're not emotionally whole. The enemy is playing mind games with you. If there is something from your past that you are still wounded from whether it be something that your mama did, your daddy did, sister, brother, nephew, auntie, grandmother, grandfather, best friend, cousin or someone who you don't know, you need to allow God to come and heal you so that you can have a stronger and more intimate relationship with Him.

I'll never forget my dad casted out demons from this young lady, afterwards she went on her way and was doing well, but it was for a short time. Her emotional issues kicked backed into gear and when me and my dad saw her we were reminded of Matthew 12:43-45,

"When an impure spirit comes out of a person, it goes through arid places seeking rest and does not find it. 44 Then it says, 'I will return to the house I left.' When it arrives, it finds the house unoccupied, swept clean and put in order. Then it goes and takes with it seven other spirits more wicked than itself, and they go in and live there. And the final condition of that person is worse than the first."

She was doing well but she didn't know how to guard against the enemy. She knew she was free but she wasn't whole. An event happened that triggered the area in which there were emotional wounds and she went back to the person who she was before and became much worse.

There is a difference between being made free and being made whole. Wholeness means not only are you free but you know how you ended up that way and because of this knowledge, you're now able (with the help of Jesus Christ who strengthens you) to guard against the enemy so that you walk in wholeness. You can be free and not be whole.

Being free means yes, you got rid of all, you're healed but, there can be a relapse.

It's important that you take care of the things of your body including things of your mind. If you don't get these areas of your life taken care of, where you actually have the skills to fight against the enemy, the skills to fight against bad habits, disappointments and un forgiveness then, the enemy will use those things as a pawn to gain access and entry in your life.

Thus, if you're a workaholic, you don't talk to anyone, you have no days off at all, all you do is work Sunday to Sunday. The enemy will then hit you with stress, he's going to provide you with more opportunities for you to work and run your body down. Here you are thinking it's God blessing you but it's the enemy setting you up like dangling a piece of meat to a hungry lion. The enemy then stops you from being a balanced person, like the Proverbs 31 woman, the woman that every Christian girl aspires to be like, a woman of balance.

- ❖ She looks after her husband (Proverbs 31:11,12;
- ❖ She is a woman who is fruitful (Proverbs 31:13,14,15;
- ❖ A woman who is sober and temperate, who doesn't rush in making

decisions (Proverbs 31:16);

- ❖ She looks after herself both spiritual and physically (Proverbs 31:17,25);
- ❖ She is a woman of substance (Proverbs 31:18);
- ❖ She is a woman of charitable works (Proverbs 31:20);
- ❖ Her home husband and kids are well taken care of (Proverbs 31:21,23,27,28);
- ❖ She is involved in ministry (Proverbs 31:26)

She wasn't so focused on one thing that she neglected the other. The enemy will set you up in the natural so that he can gain entry in the spiritual. We can make decisions in our minds, and if we are not making good decisions (taking time to seek The Lord about the decisions that we make, even the "little" decisions, not rushing in our decision making like the Proverbs 31 woman (Proverbs 31:16 being a woman who is sober) then, the enemy is going to attack us in our mind. The enemy is after your mind. If he can just control your mind, then he can control your destiny. That's why the bible says

"let this mind be in you which was in Christ."
~Philippians 2:5

That means you have to have the mind of Christ because whoever controls your mind controls your destiny. If we don't have the mind of Christ in us and if we don't take ownership of it then it gives the enemy access to control our minds and our destiny. Whenever you start getting those thoughts of doubts and fear, speak the word of God over yourself OUTLOUD! Lay hands on your head and say *"For God has not given me this spirit of fear, of doubt, He has given me a spirit of power, love and a sound mind and I take ownership of what God has given me."* To protect you from the spirit of fear, God has given you the Spirit of power, love (which by the way casts out fear according to 1 John 4:18) and a sound mind. That's 3 things to defeat 1 thing! Isn't God good? Meditate on that scripture! You have the mind of Christ!

The enemy will also work with disappointments to jack up your emotions. The main thing that enemy will go after is your mind, not your car, not your money, not your house etc. but, your mind. We as women are producers: you bring groceries to a woman, she will cook you dinner, if a man put his seed inside a woman she produces a baby. As we have discovered, the Proverbs 31 woman was a productive woman, she wasn't lazy or idle, we are favoured as women to have all these attributes. So, let's say the enemy takes £5 from you, well, you can just bind and rebuke that and produce even more because it is God who gives us power to get wealth according to Deuteronomy 8:18.

For the enemy, that's only a temporary setback, it doesn't STOP anything and what he wants to do is to completely STOP your prosperity by messing with your mind. Therefore, if you want to break the spirit of poverty, work on your mind.

Back to the trick of the enemy,

❖ 1. Disappointments
The enemy watches you all day long, he watches so that he can see your weak points (side note - people who are successful in the occult are observers of human behaviour.)
Let's say a witch comes to your church or your business etc. they will sit at the back and "discern" what's going on? Who is who? Who are the major players? What are the strongholds and weaknesses of that particular ministry or person or pastor that they are targeting and they go back to their coven and they device a plan against that. They will come to church and sound like a "lost person" who is "seeking God", they will get in the prayer line to see if someone prays for them, will they feel power. They will even get close to the gossipers in church so that they can get the ins and outs of that church. The enemy observes you, he has read your profile. So, as he watches you and observes you, he could realise that this person is

weak emotionally and then he says *"I will create some diversions."* He will then send this blocker spirit called disappointments and remember, different things disappoint different people.

Let's say someone is in bondage from the spirit of poverty, he will send lack of money. He will create some type of disappointment for you not to keep a job or every time you get money, you spend it all. You stop tithing because you've already spent it, you're already spending money before you even get the money causing yourself to be in debt then you get disappointed. That spirit literally chips away from the emotional walls (this is a mind attack) and then once that happens you start saying *"maybe God isn't my provider, God why am I going through this?"* etc. This creates a seed of doubt in your mind and once that seed of doubt is created in your mind, the enemy will say *"well I'm the father of lies, so I'm going to lie to her and tell her that God doesn't love her, she's alone, there's no hope"* and a whole lot of other lies.

You go from being a woman of confidence and strength to a woman who hasn't let go of disappointments, that bring in a spirit of doubt then the father of lies comes in and all of a sudden you're emotionally torn. You become depressed, don't believe God no more , stop going to church, and what used to be the mind of Christ, is now a mind in bondage and the devil is now controlling your destiny....BOOM!

Another example, let's say everything is all good before you enter into a relationship. So, you get into the relationship, you feel this is the one because you've been wanting to get married. You were a good steward in Christ, you were doing well, then once you get into a relationship, you focus on that relationship more than you focused on God. (Remember ladies, The Proverbs 31 Woman who we all admire was a balanced woman, like I said earlier, she wasn't so focused on one thing that she neglected the rest.)

Suddenly you look at all the failed relationships and you become disappointed because you put a person in your life who appeared great but they're damaged and you're damaged also.

When you come together as two broken people, a HUGE collision takes place. Your relationship is doomed from the very beginning because none of you are whole enough to be able to have the skills set to have and maintain a strong relationship, Your relationship becomes a target for the enemy and he will surely attack but you need to be strong enough to be able to withstand the trials and any attacks of the enemy for you are more than a conquerors.

We wouldn't be called conquerors if there was nothing to conquer. So, this experience of a bad relationship leaves with doubt, wondering how you're not going to get married, whether you'll ever have children. Eventually, you get angry at God.

"oh God, I was biggest tither, why won't you let him marry me? What's wrong with me?"

Overtime, you gain low self-esteem, everything about you, you hate and now, the enemy has your mind.

You now see people who you grew up with getting married and you get angry. Watch what disappoints you. Yes, sometimes things are not going to go our way but, it's how we handle these things emotionally that matters. Is it okay to cry? Yes, but, it's not okay for you to go on a rampage and throw a fit every time you don't get your way. That's rage and rage is a demon. It's okay to be angry but as the bible tells us, be angry but don't sin, don't let the sun go down whilst you're angry. (Ephesians 4:26) It's okay to be angry but don't stay there.

❖ 2. Frustration and other hidden emotions

Again, the enemy is watching your human behavior. Whatever part frustrates you chips away from your mind. This spirit will hold you captive until you experience spiritual and natural paralysis. If you submit to this spirit of frustration, you will not be able to move forward spiritually because you're drenched with your own emotions. Frustration leaves you tearing up stuff in the spirit with your mouth. The spirit of frustration doesn't damage other people's lives as much as it damages yours. For example, have you ever seen people frustrated that they start tearing up their own stuff? That's exactly what happens with the spirit of frustration. It causes you to tear up what you built with your own hands.

Proverbs 14:1 *"A wise woman builds her home, but a foolish one tears it down with her own hands."*

So, now you'll spend more time apologising, repairing yourself etc. and it leaves you stagnant in a jacked up place where you constantly have to keep rebuilding what you once built. The enemy brings the spirit of frustration to literally paralyse you to the point where if you're moving forward, a "frustrating" scenario will take place. And if you have not learned to recognise the tricks of the enemy, to be able to control what's going on in your mind, then you will say and do the wrong things.

How does frustration paralyse you in the natural? Well, the evidence is in the things that you tore up, those Godly relationships that sharpened you as iron sharpens iron that you walked away from and the people you said nasty hurtful stuff to.

❖ 3. Eye gate, ear gates and actions

It's important to guard our hearts. However, some of us have barbed wire around our heart that even God Himself can't speak to you. That is a false sense of safety. When God tells us to guard our heart it means to use discernment. Anyone who is not emotionally balanced is not going to have good discernment. When you are emotionally unhealthy, you will always make unhealthy decisions and those unhealthy decisions will cause you to be even more unhealthy emotionally and more emotionally imbalanced.

The question to ask yourself is, the enemy is under your feet but, have you evicted him from your mind? If you want to be a meat eating Christian, you have got to know how to work that sword and cut up that meat, chew it up and be able to digest it.

Conclusion

On the 31st of December 2015, in the middle of my prayer, I just became still in God's presence and I heard God clearly say *"Beauty for Ashes"* three times. And I enquired of The Lord concerning this. A lot of people were coming up to me telling me that God has put a ministry on the inside of me. I didn't give it much thought because of the state I was in and also I didn't want to move based on what people said about me, I wanted God to confirm it, and on that day, He did. I'm grateful to God to be a prophetic voice, I'm grateful to God to be His mouthpiece and above all else, I am grateful to God that I am His daughter. I'm one of His sheep, and because I'm one of His sheep, I have the privilege (which I DO NOT take lightly AT ALL) to hear His voice.

For The Single Mum

I had my daughter when I was 22 on the 24th of October 2011. God is faithful to see you through. Your Heavenly Father is your strength, He is your provider, the very lover of your soul.

For every time you have felt weak, His word says His strength is made perfect in your weakness. His word says, *"Let the weak say I am strong,"* declare that you are strong in the Lord and in the power of His might. For every time you have felt lonely, Your Heavenly Father is always watching over you and your child. For every time you have been saddened by the lack of a fatherly figure for your child, His word says *He is a Father to the Fatherless.* For every time you have felt that you wouldn't have enough, His word says *He will provide ALL your needs according to His riches in Glory in Christ Jesus.*

He did it for this other single mum, this lady was pretty much homeless and her plan was to make the last bit of dinner she had for herself and her son and then both die. But God had other plans. An amazing man of God called Prophet Elijah asked her to make him some food. Even though she didn't have much and barely scraped up enough, she did it, she obeyed, and guess what?, because of her faith and obedience, her and her son lived and were never hungry again.

Never allow other people (not even yourself) to label you as a *"baby mama"* NO! You're a MOTHER and your price is far above rubies. It's important to take a look at what you're doing (or NOT doing) every single day as a parent and think of how it will shape your kid/s and their future.

To every girl, woman and lady that has ever been abused (physically, sexually &emotionally), the enemy has been after the girl child because it is the seed of that girl that will crush the head of the serpent (the serpent being mentioned here is the devil.) God cares about you, don't sit there and let the enemy play mind games with you. We read about the woman in Revelations 12 who was about to give birth to a male child who was to rule all nations with a rod, the bible also tells us that the devil was right there waiting to devour the child as soon as he was born but, God is always miles ahead of the devil. God had already prepared a place for the woman and her child. (Rev 12:5-6)

God has also prepared a place of safety for you. A place where you will be nourished, healed and restored. Once you have been nourished, healed and restored, you will be like a well-watered garden, the planting of the Lord, fruitful at ALL times! God loves you! He cares!

The vision God gave me for this ministry comes from Job 22:23 *"If you return to The Almighty, you will be built up."* - to return this hurting woman and girl back to God so that He can build her up into a woman who walks in power, authority and complete wholeness.

About The Author

Ruva Ngundu is a highly anointed, authentic prophetic voice with a mandate to preach, teach and minister healing, wholeness and deliverance to the ladies, women, girls and single mothers. Her unique, sound, authentic testimony is very much needed in this day and age. It shows God's undeniable, unfathomable, undying and perfect love which casts out fear.

Printed in Great Britain
by Amazon